CW00554505

Desert Conversation

Luke Goss

Published 2018

NEW HAVEN PUBLISHING LTD

www.newhavenpublishingltd.com

newhavenpublishing@gmail.com

Design © Pete Cunliffe

pcunliffe@blueyonder.co.uk

Photographs © Luke Goss

ISBN: 978-1-910705-98-8

Desert Conversation

Luke Goss

Solitude can be
intimidating, but
only if you have no
desire to remember
who you really are.

Desert Conversation

The question I ask myself with a mixture of excitement and curiosity is "Why do I want to be alone for four days and nights in the Joshua Tree desert? Why do I want silence and solitude so deeply that I feel almost claustrophobic in my desire to experience it?"

Three years ago, I lost my beautiful mother to cancer, and just as many of us have experienced that loss, we understand the mixed emotions that leave holes in our lives when we lose loved ones and family members. It challenges our faith and sometimes shakes us to our core; that, I am sure, is individual in each experience. For me it was the starting point of a journey that began to fill me with a deep desire to seek answers - why I am here, and what I am supposed to do with my life? I know some people might ask *"why?"* because they may think I am already doing it: fulfilling my dreams in film, acting and directing, writing books, or playing large concerts with my band, but that was not the question in my mind.

After the loss of my mother I started meditating more often, because it helped me with the grief and because a friend of mine had experienced a vivid dream, with a message telling me I should meditate more. The dreamer received that message from my late mother, so being a good son, I did as I was told. That is where my journey of self-discovery, the journey that has and is continuing to change and shape my life, began.

The past has
already done its
worst, let it go and
thrive forward

As a small boy, being raised by my mother and grandfather, I was lucky enough to be provided with the belief of healing through faith.

My grandfather was a tough, strong man, who served his country in the Second World War as a gunner and later was a head foreman on large building sites in London. He lost his wife to cancer; she was only fifty-five years of age. During this time of his life, he became aware of a gift he had: the gift of healing through faith.

So, being the wonderful man that he was, he dedicated his life to healing others without any desire to be financially rewarded for it. I can easily say my grandfather was the kindest, most loving, guiding male force in my life. This is the man who, along with his daughter - my mother - raised me.

Now, I understand that this is certainly not the usual upbringing in a tough part of South East London, but it is without doubt my most treasured peaceful memory of my life so far. The reason for sharing this is not only to inform briefly of my beginning, but to ask a question.

For me, I have recently realized that this was a time in my life when I was “the real me”. Sure, I was without life wisdom and life pain, as well as untouched by life cynicism that is bestowed upon us during the conditioning process of life, but looking back, I recognize a different kind of wisdom: the kind that is funded by truth and reflex without the conditioning of society or etiquette. My question was:

How I can find that boy within me again?

Get more followers...

continue as you are...

Get more likes...

continue as you are...

Get more love...

Give more love...

I believe we all have those times in our lives when the real us was alive and well and, most importantly, without judgment. Sure, being a kid comes with rules and regulations from adults, but there is also a brief time in our lives when we are actually free: free because our parents are also learning about us, wondering who we are and how to guide us. They guide us with their wealth of knowledge or lack thereof, so we slowly become conditioned by their belief system or life standpoint. From that moment, I believe, we move away from our true selves. Not because our parents are doing anything wrong; in their own way they are helping us prepare for the big wide world, which is something we need to do in order to function as members of a society that certainly isn't getting any kinder or easier. In fact, my personal observation is that the world is becoming so driven by ego and consumption that we are not only losing our ability to interact, but more importantly, we are losing our ability to be available to help one another.

So, back to my little desert trip.

I am packed and ready for my drive alone to the desert, excited with my gadgets to help make the experience a little more comfortable: lanterns, a little heater, glow sticks, a large knife, firewood - and lots of it, as it gets extremely cold at night this time of year out there, thermals and boots, and all the usual stuff that makes going out to nature fun.

I load up the car, excited like a child, ready to finally get to a place of peace and quiet, especially after spending the last seven months being followed daily by a documentary crew who were making a feature film about me and my brother: the story

None of us live
forever on this
plane but the love
we leave will grant
us all immortality

behind the story of our beginning and of our band Bros. They are a great bunch of people and are great at what they do, but, that said, like anything for public consumption, it must be entertaining, so there is always an agenda. Of course, they as documentarians want a film that will be captivating and watchable. While I, being a filmmaker myself, certainly understand that, it wasn't until the process was underway that I realized I was in the middle of a new existence - an existence where it was a daily goal for the crew to unpick me and reveal cracks in my wall: a wall we all have, where we compartmentalize our pain and suffering, so we can endure life itself.

It was a realization that this movie might as well be a defining insight into me, yet there was a huge part that was not being told. Not because I was hiding it, but because, like all of us, I needed to keep something for myself. Sure, the person I was while being filmed is the man I am, but not *all* the man I am. So, I already knew that not all of myself would be seen, and that is one of the reasons I am using this trip to not only share that side of me, but also with a deep hope that by writing this little book, at least one person will relate to it and feel less alone, less overwhelmed or afraid, knowing that they are not alone in their peaceful heart or compassionate nature, in a world where selfies are more important than being conscious, or kind, or supportive, or even simply present.

In no way am I saying this in a judgmental manner, but rather as an acknowledgement that, at this time in our history, if we don't conform to the noise of social media, for example, and enhance digitally our already beautiful selves, we will fall short of the popularity stakes. However, I believe all of our

Turning hate into
love is energetic
alchemy, and
equally miraculous.

imperfections, as they are perceived in this harsh day and age, are exactly what make us so bloody perfect and so very unique. What saddens me is the fact that we live in a time when being kind publicly is less interesting than posting a woman falling off a stage or an elderly man slipping over in a parking lot. Watch the number of views on a clip that is in essence funded by ridicule, alongside an encouraging post; it will be one hundred to one in favor of ridicule or judgment.

So, that said, the motivation behind my trip was to ask myself this following question:

"What can I do that allows me to feel authentic, and still be a participant in life without compromising my core values or my simple desire to be kind and encouraging, and to strive daily, even if it's a tiny bit - to improve myself as a contributing human being?"

As I get close to the campground where I will be staying for the next four days, I get more excited - knowing the trip I had been waiting for is minutes away from its beginning.

I pull over into the dusty road and park my car in front of a wooden entrance; there is no bordering fence of any kind, just a bull's skull and a tepee to my left. My tent is about a football pitch in length away, so I begin taking the wood I have bought, bit by bit, to my beautiful home for four days and nights: a white canvas tent. The retreat I have chosen is peaceful and beautiful, and since no other guests booked the week, I am happy to know I will be alone, without temptation to befriend anyone and actually feel less guilt about what felt

We are but a
candle but I must
contribute to the
light that will
eventually prevail

at this time to be a selfish desire, but a deeply needed one.

As a celebrity, finding time for self is just as hard as it is for all of us. That might be due to our busy lifestyles or a lack of disposable income, responsibilities, family, or just simply because we don't feel deserving of a trip dedicated to alone time; maybe because we don't want our significant others to feel they are not welcome. I am sure, for all of us, there are many reasons we don't seek solitude in our own lives.

I think one reason for this is because we are all addicts in a way: addicts to Facebook or e-mail or texts or Twitter or Instagram or Snapchat or food or booze or drugs or porn or whatever thing it is that is so perfectly designed to distract us, distract us from something wonderful, something capable of getting us closer to God regardless of a chosen faith, closer to the one thing that can truly assist us in having a happier, more peaceful, more abundant, more authentic life - ourselves.

***

After the following two hours going back and forth to the car for supplies, chopping wood for the cold night ahead, and putting on the new thermals and boots, I finally sat down as the sun began to set. For the first time in my entire life, I was sitting totally alone in a place without anyone around me and nobody in sight, the Joshua trees all around as my only companions. I smiled and felt truly lucky to be sitting here, so I said a quick prayer of gratitude.

Look at the light in the world
and be a mirror to that

Meditation or stillness allows us to know who we are and how to bring happiness to our own lives and in turn share that happiness with everyone around us

One hour later, the sun had set and the desert chill was well and truly underway. I lit my fire earlier than I needed because I was still in a place of excitement, and like anyone who has spent time in nature knows, a campfire is a very comforting part of the experience. Later I realized that firewood is not something to be squandered because the sooner you light it, the sooner you burn through it, and running out of wood is no fun on a night when you can see your own breath, mixed with a mild icy breeze that doesn't let up often at this time of year.

So began my first night alone.

At first I tried to ignore my fears. I am a tough boy and there is no place for that, but after only a few hours I realized that I would leave this beautiful place without a lesson if I didn't own my fears. Lessons come during silence, and fear is the loudest of all the noise that fills our minds. I asked myself the obvious question:

What am I afraid of? What is making me feel so uneasy? Why am I not simply enjoying this unique experience?

It was unfamiliar and different; I was alone without distraction or counsel from anyone: just me, my faith, and my demons to keep me company. I realized almost immediately that was why I was here.

Now, I must say I have such deep gratitude and appreciation for every effort in every case: for help and guidance I have received throughout my life, but being a celebrity, even as I sat here alone in the cold dark desert, I could feel an almost judging

A kind act creates a chain reaction,
a reaction that can be forever enduring
- go ahead and start yours.

Your light will
brighten the
darkness

energy. Things like "He's such a hippy" or "He's going through a phase" sprang to my mind. That might not be the dialogue spoken in my absence, yet I felt this nagging guilt about being me: simple, peaceful, compassionate, but still... within the world I live, I was aware that my nature was under question and scrutiny.

It was around midnight when I calmed my mind from the cacophony of thoughts and worries and doubts and fears. I said aloud to myself "Stop, Luke, just stop and really listen! That is why you are here!" It was a firm outburst that came from nowhere, but I recognized it was exactly what I should do, so I did as I was told, maybe from a higher source, or maybe from my true self feeling impatient with my inability to tone down the noise within me; I listened to the guidance being offered and sat still for the next hour in complete silence.

During that hour the red moon broke the horizon, and almost immediately this city boy found himself in the dark with a campfire, watching the red moon, larger than I can ever remember seeing it and accompanied by what sounded like dozens of coyotes howling as if their lives depended on it. I remember actually laughing and thinking to myself *God certainly knows exactly how to up the stakes and make a challenge more effective.* It felt like I was being asked spiritually *"Are you really ready for the next four days out here alone?"* That was the point where I knew that, no matter how uncomfortable or uneasy I felt, I wasn't going home early. So I sat still, allowing myself to feel uneasy with the rustling noises behind me, while the kangaroo rats made their incessant visits to me without rest, in search for my gifts of cashew nuts or whatever had fallen onto the desert floor.

I remember thinking about a Youtube video clip I love: The Samurai and the Fly. I realized that, even though I had spent years in the pursuit of acceptance and release of fear, that was exactly what I was doing now: sure, I was listening to everything in and outside of my mind, but always with an irrational degree of fear, instead of letting it all just be.

Knowing this wasn't going to be a one-night fix, at 4 a.m., after attempting my usual late night mediation by the fire, I decided that it was time for bed. As I lay there with my boots off, which for a city boy just didn't feel right at first because I didn't feel ready to jump up and defend myself from the multitude of villains I had created in my mind, slowly and with one ear open, I finally drifted off to sleep.

***

Waking up on my first morning here felt great because I knew I still had three days and nights left. I separate them because one thing I learned about being isolated in nature is that the day experience is profoundly different from the night experience, yet both bring their own degree of insight and learning. After boiling some water, I made coffee with my French press, adding a little more heavy cream than necessary, and as I had promised myself, I started my day of silence.

My first feeling upon waking up was excitement about the outdoor shower the retreat had installed in a small outbuilding nearby my tent. Being the only one here, I allowed myself to enjoy a longer than needed shower, taking time to feel the sun wash my body simultaneously with the water. I prayed as I washed myself, attempting to clean my

body not only of dirt, but also of negative and toxic energy. I felt joyful because nobody was there to view me as crazy or obsessed. However, as I write this, I feel I did have an obsession this morning with cleansing, but it felt liberating and energizing.

The day was warmer than the day before, so I chopped some wood for the fire, ate light, and moved slowly. I slept in the hammock and allowed my thoughts, as I said I would, to be there without debate: almost like meditation, where I let my thoughts behave like clouds passing in the wind. Sure, I observe them, but I let them go their way without curiosity, and more importantly, without worry or fear.

Something I had on my to-do list was to walk a while barefoot on the desert floor to connect with Mother Earth. So, I took off my boots and socks and spent the following few hours feeling the floor of the desert through the soles of my feet.

One reason I did this is because while feeling the sandy gravel barefoot, I felt less disconnected to simplicity and less connected to the fear of the fire ants or scorpions or whatever was wandering the floor of the desert. In reality it is their turf; they own it, and I am a guest here. With this thought I started my first moment of acceptance of my new, albeit brief, place of residence.

For me that was one of the points of all this.

I don't like the uneasy feeling which many of the changes in the world that showed up so quickly, so abruptly, make me feel. Without any caution or question, the world grabs onto every distraction and every fear with both hands. Here in the desert

I found myself thinking about how I interacted with myself and the effort I had to make to get myself away from all the things that on a daily basis distract me from me, not to mention the people both in my private world and the world itself.

I asked myself:
"Has it really reached a point where trolls have more power than God in some people's lives, and do hateful appalling acts of terrorism really run the world now?"

I don't write that in a disrespectful way to anyone's faith, but because we, as a society, a society that absolutely has the power to change things, should demand a standard from our fellow humans, and not turn a blind eye to prejudice or arrogance, ego, rudeness, bullying trolls or superficial standards that, frankly, I feel are out of control.

These are just my thoughts, but again, I am inclined to write them in hope that maybe a few of us can prioritize these things and ask ourselves the following question: *when did it become so uncool to be kind?* Why can we be inspired and excited in the kitchen when looking at other cultures, and see new ways or lessons in how to make a wonderful recipe, yet our possessiveness hinders our acceptance and ability to learn from our planet and its multilayered beliefs and cultures?

I see world leaders, many with ambition and careers maybe seeking a voice in history. Some achieve it through dictatorship and death, but their legacy is not enduring through history; they come and go, leaving their ego and all of its destruction for us to clean up. I often have a desire to ask the leaders of the world a simple question...

Do you not see that the immortality you seek is so much more likely to be achieved if you and your fellow leaders realize that by bringing peace to Earth your legacy would be forever enduring?

So, even if it appeals to an ego or two, I hope one day that will be the motive for our leaders to conspire together to achieve not only a better planet for us all, but a legacy that is actually worth dedicating a life to. The men and women who make this a reality will be forever the foundation of a brighter present and future; they will be infinitely loved not only by the country they represented, but by the entire planet, forever.

Idealistic? Absolutely. But dreams are not nurtured by pragmatic submission.

What are we afraid of? Maybe human nature wants to be right, yet I can't help but wonder why can we not learn from conflict and be more accepting of each other on all levels? I am so frustrated with the fact that we abide by the rules of hate presented by conflict. I believe we must consider a simple idea before looking at our enemy in war: imagine a young boy or girl covered in dust and blood, not just their own blood, but the blood of their dead loved ones, killed by a bomb or attack. It is not important what side one sees, because as that young child grows up with that image in their mind, is their suffering, as they see the disfigured face of their mother and father, brother and sister before them, any less awful or tragic?

Your dreams are
limited only by
what you can hold
in your heart and
imagination

No matter whose side that child is on, did they personally ask for that conflict or death? They too at that stage of life are a victim. What happens from then is hate, anger, resentment and fear, all conspiring to encourage and elongate suffering and war. We must all defend our families, of course, but we must remember why we fight, and be sure we fight the aggressors of peace, never the innocent.

We are one race on one planet, and I pray one day we will realize there are more of us who want peace than war, but that will never happen without that single race breathing through past anger and hate, knowing our composure will spare the lives of many if we do so.

Is it more painful to face your fears, or live the life fear will give you?

***

My second day was joyful, questions appeared from unknown places; I decided to do what I am currently doing because of them, writing this little book of thoughts. What at first had seemed to be nothing more than private contemplation of my mind, jotted down for personal reflection, now called for a more substantial purpose. As the day was drawing to an end, I watched the fire-red sky come to life yet again. I jumped up to get my iPhone tripod and remote to document my experience, not knowing if it would be just for myself, or if there was a bigger point to it. I spent the next hour enjoying cactus and skylines. I was happy and thankful for the privilege of this experience.

Let us be the
generation that
makes love our
global religion

In my enthusiasm I had not prepared a fire while I could still see, so I layered up everything once again and waited an hour longer to preserve my firewood; otherwise, I would have to face the world sooner than I had intended, to acquire more. Not wanting to leave the desert before my time was up, I was more aware on this second night to use the firewood more sparingly.

That in itself made me consider another subject: consumption.

Sure, we all love new things and why not? However, there comes a point when I see people standing in the rain in front of a store, without any courtesy from that same store to offer its customers comfort or shelter as they make them wait to take their money for a product that is in essence a fraction of an improvement of the same object they hold in their hand.

Why? Because life itself, not just our work, has become a competitive environment that is the perfect fertilizer to grow and nurture addiction: an addiction that is, in my humble opinion, hurting all of us in a way we are failing to see, all for the chance, all be it brief, to have the newest or latest, even if the improvements are negligible. Basic courtesy and care for each other, as well as respect for each other, including retailers, should be an expectation from all of us - because if we give up our right to be treated in a respectful way, where will we end up? What will we be getting for our hard-earned money?

Consumption is limiting our potential and it is something that transcends our need for gadgets and inanimate objects; it affects our bodies as much as it affects our minds. Food, health and wellbeing are, in my opinion, at a place of disgrace. There is now scientific proof that our over-consumption of food is creating a catastrophic health crisis, with cancer being more prevalent than ever.

Recently I watched a documentary called 'The Science Of Fasting". It presented the idea that fasting actually benefits our bodies, and studies have shown that when a sixty-hour fast is implemented before chemotherapy, it reduces side effects dramatically, allowing for higher doses of chemotherapy to be administered. The study in the film has shown that fasting makes the healthy cells go into protective mode, allowing them to be significantly less affected by the indiscriminate poison used to kill the cancer; this allows the healthy cells to live, helping the patient recover with more hope and fewer side effects.

My mother might have benefited from this, but wasn't given a chance to even try it. I am sure there are many of us out there who would look at all options when trying to save the life of someone we love; that I believe is our right and our reflex.

Now, I understand this study may have accurate and inaccurate statements - but my point is, we must stay open to different and new ways of thinking, and not allow the unknown to be greeted with cynicism, for that itself is pure fear and that fear will negate our opportunity to learn.

In Japan there is a thirty-year study proving that water has memory. On a molecular level water has the ability to remember and respond to positive words and affirmations, just as it responds

Sometimes the
noise of life is
louder than our
dreams, take a
moment to hear
them again.

negatively to insults or hurtful words. This is a scientifically proven fact.

Think about that; we ourselves are made of approximately 75% water, so how are we any different when receiving good or bad energy or language? If anything could aid us in healing, it would be water; and yet, in our overconsumption of food, soft drinks, and alcohol, we often don't even remember to drink enough water in order to hydrate and fuel our bodies with the very liquid that keeps us alive.

We are hunter-gatherers, and throughout history our thriving race benefited from less consumption. Eating less allows our stomach to rest and can alleviate, or even reverse, depression, as well as common problems like arthritis, high blood pressure, anxiety, high cholesterol, and so many other conditions we all live with, and for which we are fed pills that only mask symptoms, but provide no real healing benefits.

We have become dependent on prescription drugs, which benefits the medical industry more than it benefits our health. Healthcare has become a business, and the profound reasonability of the medical field has been hijacked by the business of medicine that has long lost its origins of healing. Processed, synthetic foods, pesticides and convenience are now the foundation for some individuals in power to use for profit, somehow overlooking its affect on all of us. I feel that is a sin and a tragedy.

Now, this is not a political point I am making; it is an observation of something that hurts me because I know that a reduction of consumption can literally help those with ailments and sickness. It can even help those feeling lost or abandoned through depression. Lack of awareness about this hurts, because I myself lost my mother to a disease that is ravaging our families and friends daily, but no healing is being offered from simple low-cost alternatives because that harms business, and that hurts my heart.

I am not saying that thousands of men and women in the medical field are less frustrated by the awful fact that business has become the leading edge in medicine, but I am calling out for an awareness of the possibility that something as simple as a reduction in consumption and the magic of water can do more for our wellbeing than we could have ever imagined. There is nothing wrong with learning or adjusting our beliefs if the new information helps us as a society, right?

Think about this for a second: if someone raises a point that is only considering the wellbeing of one's neighbor with no financial or commercial benefit, then maybe it is funded by an honest desire to illuminate complimentary options that might just save a life or two, so why not go investigate yourself? Now everything can be proven or disproven, but without inquiry we will remain like a herd, and I believe with all I am that we deserve better.

Unfortunately, without a mass demand for better, more truthful options for our wellbeing we will simply become more conditioned and more sick.

Obviously this is a much broader point; it is about decency and humanity.

If we don't see and learn that addictions are ruling our lives, if we don't stand up and start expecting more for our lives, if we keep feeding feverishly, I can't help but wonder what will happen when we run out of things to distract us from ourselves and the ones we love? What will be left for our children and grandchildren?

Will anyone open a door for a woman again? Even though she is obviously more than capable of opening it herself. Will we just speak of a time where an elderly man or woman or a person with a disability is, of course, given a seat on the train or bus? Or will it remain a time when lessons are not given by example - from a generation that still remembers civility and compassion: a time when we just watch silently as a young man or woman sit and stare at their phone, unable to interact or even notice the person struggling to stand and suffering on a bus, while they sit on an app, isolating themselves from life and its point for the duration of their existence, devoid of empathy or sympathy? What kind of a standard will there be in twenty years?

I ask this as I sit here without distraction in the desert, about to light my firewood to stay a little warmer tonight - and so my second night begins.

It is eight o'clock in the evening; it has been dark for only two hours, but it feels like four. Again I am surprised by the *peace* of silence. Knowing from the previous night some of the noises to expect, I feel less on edge and more a part of the desert. As the previous night, the coyotes are making themselves known. Tonight their presence offers a little comfort. It is a tiny piece of evolution: something that evoked an uneasy feeling the night

BRAND

Luke Goss

before, something unknown that triggered even a small bit of fear, a fear that might generate an unnecessary response to something that has no intention whatsoever to harm me, is the very thing that offers comfort this night.

I can't help but wonder if that could apply to people who have been conditioned or taught prejudice.

From my personal observation, I believe we are taught hate and prejudice from a place of fear; it certainly isn't something we are given by God at birth. What strikes me as strange is the fact that we live our lives wanting something new, not old or used, yet some welcome old hatred or second-hand prejudice with open arms. New, bright ideas and views fall on deaf ears.

We embrace all science without question, especially about New Age or ethereal beliefs, even though we have been shown throughout history that knowledge is constantly being adjusted to accommodate new science which makes obsolete previous knowledge.

Quantum physics, flight, medicine, and knowledge about the universe are just a few examples which might help us understand that the change of knowledge is the universe's way of showing us that we must have open minds and that an open mind must not be afraid of new contradicting knowledge, including the joy or love you have for your neighbour's culture or skin colour, even if it contradicts what you have been taught. Courage to stand up for what you know is right comes from the recognition that truth is as it is, and even fear should not sway your judgment.

It is wonderful being silent, alone and away from one's comfort zone, because you are given two choices: evolve, or leave as you were, without improvement or growth. I never knew being out here would offer so many thoughts about so many topics.

Also, I had no idea that the environment itself would offer metaphors and examples which relate directly to another world of creature comforts, addiction, noise, and distraction. The more I am here, the happier I am to be here.

The fire is getting low, so I add one more piece of wood, and enjoy the flickering flames and crackling sounds. Tonight, with less fear, I close my eyes for about twenty minutes and start my second night of meditation.

I have been dedicated to my own personal meditation technique for about three years now. As I mentioned before, I took to heart a friend's dream with my mother's instructions to meditate more, and I am so deeply thankful for the place meditation now has in my life. Meditation, for me, is truly the catalyst that has assisted me back to a place of faith, not religion.

Now, I respect everyone's religious beliefs if it offers comfort and encourages peace. For me though, I have never felt comforted by established religions because I have seen too many examples of man's input and manipulation of religion for their own benefit to feel trusting of it. That said, I do love the wisdom and comforting guiding words of Buddha, and I do love Christ and pray to God, but in my very own personal and somewhat simple approach.

With closed eyes, we are all
colorless. Opening them should
illuminate, not create hate.

True Faith is
Knowing,
knowing is peace.

I was, for a brief time in my childhood, educated in a Church school just outside London: St. Clement's Church School. Personally, I always felt a sense of mourning and sadness, as well as a fear, when I was in service. Now I recognize it wasn't fear at all, but more a discipline. When I was in church, it made me feel tense and not at all peaceful; as a child that released a discomfort and fear within me.

It was a sensation which opposed my grandfather's energy of love and healing through God without the discipline of man in God's name, so for me, I would always pray while alone or in a place that I trusted.

As I got older, I would observe the money that some organisations would generate from people's sincere and honest faith, and I would feel both hurt and bothered by it. I would see churches on my travels and feel almost a sense of hierarchy within them, almost a social grading: rich hats at the front, and the less connected or wealthy at the back. Now just to explain, I am describing my own experiences and not generalizing, of course.

That said, I prayed less as I got older and witnessed, as my life unfolded, an almost uncool subject develop, a distrust from my peers and friends for organised religion. I too felt somewhat betrayed by the profit of faith that many were enjoying. I watched advertisements on TV with requests for money from people who needed help from the church, and seeing them stripped of the few coins that lined their humble pockets exacerbated my distrust as a young man.

It made me withdraw from religion, losing my connection to my faith for many years.

Meditation changed that for me; I will explain why. During my practice of meditation I have slowly learned to not only calm my body and mind, but also realized that in that state of peace and centeredness, I found questions being raised about subjects of previous heartache or moments of pain or foolishness that were presented in my silent state, a state when you are almost forced to address yourself.

Over the next three years I had many beautiful, and to be honest, etherial experiences which gave me a new gift: the gift of faith, a private and simple faith that most certainly felt nothing like the disciplinarian faith I was shown by the school I attended as a child. It felt more like a faith funded by the love my grandfather had shown me, not by words or rules, but by example.

Now I see and recognize, even with many of my friends to this day, that faith has become a subject which brings an almost uncomfortable energy with it, and I understand why. As I sit here in the dark, I wonder if there is anyone else out there looking for a deeper and more nourishing comfort from our personal beliefs or viewpoint. I feel the strong presence of man in religion and seek an energy that might actually be of benefit to my life.

I am also aware of the beautiful Churches out there and the wonderful people who are a part of them. On my travels over the last thirty years I have seen so very many examples of God at work from all colours of skin and all types of religion. For me personally, I found it hard to say this man or woman is wrong about his or her faith because I personally could see God in them through their acts of love or kindness.

Solitude is not something to fear, it is something essential and needed for our souls to be heard. Only then will pain become a lesson that can guide your next step forward.

These experiences spoke to me and instilled a belief that God is everywhere, and if one witnesses acts of goodness, kindness, or compassion, then for me I always see God in that moment. So, it would be impossible to suggest a belief system is wrong if it functions from a place of love and kindness.

Meditation simply gave me the best environment to find that simple connection again: that wonderfully comforting place within. That is truly the closest I have ever felt to the comforting presence of God.

No, I am not fanatical about it, although when I first started to awaken spiritually, especially after years without it, the enthusiasm did flow vigorously for a while, but as I now live with it daily, it is becoming something intertwined within myself and my daily life, not something I am verbose about particularly, but rather something that resonates with me and within me.

If I were to offer one suggestion to anyone out there dealing with worry, stress, deep anxiety, fears, depression, or deep pain from any source, it is that meditation will absolutely help you. It won't be achieved in a day, but if a dedication is given to it for even twenty minutes each day or night, the benefits will surprise and uplift you.

One thing I know is that for the rest of my life I will always be an encouraging force - encouraging meditation, because I know it will help people escape not only the condition of life and the stress it can bring, but also reset and replenish many parts of one's existence, and even heal more than one might think.

Looking for strength
is important, finding it
is essential

Religion, unlike meditation, can feel almost like another pressure or avenue to fall short with, but meditation will offer each and every person their very own and personal supportive connection to source energy and their own relationship with their faith, a relationship that will help them feel less alone, less afraid of death, and less fearful overall, just as it did for me.

Because of the benefits I received, I want to at least suggest it to those in need or people feeling desperate with nowhere to turn: meditation will help you.

I guess the main motive for sharing these thoughts within is to offer a gentle suggestion to those overwhelmed by this physical experience called life.

As my campfire looks sleepy and ready to turn in, I follow its lead and tidy my little camp with my flashlight in hand. I zip up my tent and head to another chilly night of sleep, still with one ear open.

***

Ego is poor soil when
trying to cultivate
a fruitful tree.

It is my third morning in the desert, and I woke up with the awareness that I only have two days and nights left to get something from this experience that I can actually take home with me. I make my morning coffee and let my body awake slowly and without a schedule for a change.

I start to feel more familiar with the environment I am in, which makes me realize that my internal monologue and the silence I sought was actually being hindered by my own noise. I become aware that unless I can let go of that noise in my mind and feel safe and fear-free, I will leave this place with nothing of use.

This day being the warmest by far, I decided to have a vacation day where I would sleep and rest without guilt; yes, guilt simply about doing nothing. Another question came to me as I had the fortunate opportunity to lay in a hammock with only thoughts and sleep on my to-do list for the day.

Maybe it was because as a working class boy, always being the breadwinner and knowing it was my responsibility to keep myself and my family safe, that I had been conditioned to worry; this was something that had clearly proved itself to be utterly worthless.There was not one single moment in my life when I could remember a benefit from fear or worry.

As I lay in the sun considering that thought, I realized worry and fear had made my life's journey harder and more arduous. It also raised an important question: *if I really did have faith of any kind, what should I be afraid of?*

That thought, today on my third day, was a turning point for me, because it adjusted very quickly the focus of my trip. Before becoming aware of this question, I had found myself being overwhelmed by the noise in my head, generated by life and all the things I have mentioned.

I noticed that we don't hear this noise while immersed in our daily existence because our environment has literally created a world where we are discouraged to find inner peace or any kind of sanctuary that isn't funded by some kind of distraction because that isn't good for business: a business where a confused state of mind is encouraged, as is the noise that pulls us all into a competitive existence, rather than one of evolution and the ability to be without distraction.
At the moment of this realization I felt a huge

sense of peace. I understood now that I had decided to come to the Joshua Tree alone for a reason, instead of going on a fancy trip with more distractions.
I felt that I had listened to the guidance for a change, embracing the opportunity to organize my mind after months of being followed by a film crew, or keeping promotional schedules, or filming movies and moving with changing environments without familiar faces to comfort me.

It had been like this for the last thirty years, and it was an existence devoid of sanctuary: a sanctuary that was not out of reach but out of sight, because I had not given priority to my solitude. Silence was the missing link. Not because silence in itself was the answer, but because silence gave me a platform to let the spinning wheels stop.

If you find yourself in
a room where
kindness isn't cool,
leave the room.

Of course, that does not happen in a day or even two, but here on this third day I started to think less about the daily grind, and more about what was the main issue, and that issue is why I am here: fear, fear, and more fear. It is, I believe, something we all feast on daily, even if we don't realize it. It feeds our insecurities; it feeds our doubts and worries in every corner of our minds. It is something that, at times, has no remedy or antivenom.

However, lying here in my hammock, gazing at the open desert sky, I start to see how comforting silence can be. It has already raised the important question: *if one has true faith, not religion but faith, can fear truly exist?*

My answer, even before I debate it, is "No, it can't."

I knew this already because I can remember moments in my life, especially recently, where I didn't have fear, and in those moments of peace, where the experience of joy or happiness was also underscored with a knowing and a sense of being on a path or journey that was absolutely meant to be, in that peace a fear-free memory existed; so, I knew that while, of course, comfort comes from our loved ones, it also must be accompanied by a sense of knowing: knowing that we are all protected, all guided, and all of us, when filled with gratitude and love, even in the struggle of life, are given the opportunity to be free from fear when we listen to that guidance.

While I write these words, I don't know if anyone will ever read them and wonder if there is any point to it, and like many of us, I wonder what ridicule or attack they might generate. I am not trying to be profound or clever; I am writing as a catharsis - to

If emotional pain
were pleasurable
we would seek it
rather than strive
to grow from it.

calm myself and address the things in the world I live in that hurt or bother me.
All the time I hear people say how lonely they are, or how isolated they feel, yet as adults we have moved beyond the school playground and are now functioning members of our relative cultures and countries. Nevertheless, I can't help but wonder, have we found ourselves in a new kind of playground with the same issues of bullying and censorship? I believe we are currently in a tougher, more brutal, more disruptive and abusive playground than ever before.

Look at your phone and consider its use; it is a communication device. However, most of its time in your hand it is used not only for checking e-mails and messages, but also for checking every avenue of social media and touching base with the daily list of apps and distractions that actually have nothing to do with communication at all.

As a selfie is taken, and eyes are whitened and faces adjusted, the photo posted and left to gather compliments or ridicule, we are being encouraged by the apps, sure, but more by the human desire to be accepted. Yet, what is accepting about a self image that has been adjusted specifically to attract validation or sometimes ridicule?

Posts we hope will generate a positive response are delivered for consumption with the nagging consideration of how they might be greeted by either followers or trolls alike. Power that should be firmly in our own hands and the underscore of our self-esteem are now, whether we like it or not, in the hands of millions of unknown faces that comment on our life, our appearance, our philosophies, our spiritual beliefs, and so on.

When feeling hurt,
wait and be sure
your next action is
funded by love.

But what do we really get in return?

I guess my obvious frustration comes from the knowledge that we, as a society, are the only ones who can change this state of isolation we are all being encouraged to take part in. Think about it: the new platform for social media or the new app has been designed to pull you in; it has been designed to trigger yet another competitive instinct we all have as humans, but not one from our inner selves, not one from our better nature.

This is worrisome, and the control element that I see so very clearly hurts me. It hurts me because I see a future where we are so consumed by the next engineered distraction that we literally no longer have the courage to self-censor our consumption and demand the developers of the latest and greatest new virtual experience to give us something more, something that might actually encourage good, respectful interactions and find a new smart way to make that cool. I can't help but believe I would be waiting a very long time for that.

So, it is up to us, like-minded loving, caring people, to make that change and be voices of kindness and love. Regardless of fame or money, we can all contribute in our own way to say *"NO, I won't allow ridicule; no, I won't allow bullying; no, I won't accept it, and I won't join in."*

It is a strange sensation, feeling so much pain from a subject some might think pales into insignificance when compared to issues such as gun laws or prejudice or terrorism or politics, but I believe if we don't connect literally with each other's cultures and each other, how can we have love or compassion for each other? Without those

Live in the present
enough to know the
end is too close to
waste life on hate.

elements in us we will lose our ability to actually experience empathy, and our world will become a world of apathy; that, for me, is potentially a tragedy that has evoked this writing.

It is two o'clock in the morning, and I decide to add more wood to the fire than I should, so I can stay warm longer and enjoy the sounds of the desert, letting that knot of anxiety in my stomach slowly untie. So, with the cold air whistling around me, I move to sit closer to my fire, close my eyes, and for the next forty-five minutes allow my mind to empty and just be, be with nature and the universe.

Here, in the desert, time moves at a different pace than in the city and the awareness of it melts together with silence, silence which makes the measuring construct of the modern world fade to unimportance. Why do we feel such need to measure things? Do we really "measure" time, or do we make it?

At 4 a.m. I decide it is time for bed, knowing tomorrow will be my last day here. I tell myself "Tomorrow is a day without agenda, without plan; a day I will let it unfold as it may, without curiosity or a desire to shape it. I will simply let it unfold."

The feeling tonight is different because, as I am drifting off to sleep, I am without worry or curiosity about the many noises that underscore this experience, and I already know they would become the very things I will miss when back in the dog-eat-dog world of Los Angeles.

I crack a glow stick and allow the sound of my usual music of Native American flute ease me to sleep.

Love today,
heal tomorrow.

***

Today being day four, and my final day out here, I feel a feeling of genuine gratitude, but, as I thought I would, also a feeling of sadness, knowing I will soon have to leave this brief hippy hideaway. That said, I am also aware that today and tonight is the last chance I have to really get something from this alone time, other than addressing the noise of life and the frustrations that sometimes deafen my sanctuary.

Today is a day when I should look at love and the power of it in my life.

Despite it being a brisk morning, I head for the outdoor shower. It is another wonderful purifying experience as the sun's rays blend with water once again to cleanse far beyond the dirt that covers my skin. Being heated is a luxury that I have no problem with after my chilly night.

After stepping out of the shower, I walk back to my desert home and sit down in front of my tent, allowing my mind to be at peace.

As I sit calmly, observing the scenery before me, taking in even more detail of my surroundings, I feel one thought fill my mind, one energy, and that is love, and the woman who has held it for thirty years of my adult life, my wife - a very loving special woman, a strong woman who came into my life while I was recording my first album in Fulham in London, my home town.

I have been the recipient of her guidance and support in all my endeavours, regardless of the potential outcome; even if that meant failing, I knew I had that support.

Let us not allow hate
to put its hook in our
mouths but let us
swim free in the
ocean of love and
support of each other.

Love is something I believe is a reflex, a need, and without it we wither.

However, this thought also raised the question: *are we loved for who we are, or for who we have created* - not created with a fake agenda, but created through life? Some of us are blessed to be raised, as we say in London, "born with a silver spoon in our mouths", born into a family that has the ability to help financially. I was not born with that option and am actually thankful for it because it has instilled a tenacity within me that has certainly helped me endure some of the challenges I have faced in my life, knowing I really am the only one who can fix this. Now. because of my faith. I of course know there is more than me, but I also know that, with or without the silver spoon, life is challenging for all of us, and love will surely make the hardest day more bearable and more do-able.

After my contemplation I realized that, just like the changing knowledge in science or medicine, we as individuals also evolve and make obsolete some, or even all, of our previous selves. Now, that doesn't mean the new version is not deeply connected to its original state, and in fact might actually be closer to it than ever before, closer to the being we were created to be, and probably the essence of what generated the love we have in our lives in the first place.

Change can be intimidating or even disruptive, but like buying a new car, we learn the new and improved features and handling capabilities. We don't question them because we look at them as improvements, not as something to fear or to be disturbed by.

How easily we
forget our mistakes
when we judge
others

When some of us awaken to any degree, we find ourselves also learning the new and improved features, and just like a car, we have days when we don't know how something works. With a new vehicle we simply look at the operating manual. Unfortunately, that isn't an option with ourselves, so there will be days of confusion or doubt, or even the consideration we are *losing it*.

In reality, we are simply growing, simply striving for an upgrade or evolution within ourselves, and many times that desire to evolve is not something we were consulted about, but rather something that landed within us. It is not a choice to desire evolution; I believe evolution is delivered from a higher source, and, for that reason, it is something specifically designed to make us better within, and certainly something we should not fear.

The question raised was the following: *If it is confusing for me experiencing this awakening, then how confusing must it be for those who love me while they observe this change?*

It must feel like someone changing the channel while you are watching a great movie just before the ending. I imagine it must be frustrating and annoying, and maybe, with regards to a relationship, something a little scary. From my point of view I see and understand this, and being a man who would never want to evoke hate or fear or anger, it is deeply painful to think change might cause pain.

It can be almost tempting to abandon the pursuit of change because of it.

Hate negates
the opportunity
to learn.

As I tidy my tent and start organizing my camp, wanting to make the time to leave easier, I see that my being here really was for a reason: a reason to write this catharsis and to inform myself of myself today - not of the exterior shell I have been carrying and using as an ambassador for most of my adult life, but of the newer version of myself that has been educated by life and the observation of it.

Sometimes as a victim and sometimes as a conquerer, but always from within myself, I have traveled this experience we call life. A self that has now taken charge, and demands a broader, more open interior, while still the same man, the same person, and if anything, a person with a desire for the better version of myself to be the leading edge: a version where fear or acceptance of mediocracy are no longer something I can encourage, accept, or live with.

I was wondering if it is, for those who love me, a time they might consider that I have lost my mind or become obsessed with this pursuit of growth. In reality it was fear; that I understood, because as I looked into the eyes of my new adversary, I have realized while being here that those around me have also been forced to accept it; my adversary was change itself.

As I mentioned before, using a car as an example, I have realized that change is absolutely the essence of growth and evolution, and as scary as it is, if it benefits your soul, harms nobody, and encourages love, it is nothing to be afraid of, even if it is unfamiliar. With patience, support, and an open mind you and your loved ones might even be witnesses to a better, brighter, more vibrant version

of your old self: a self that can see the pain of others, even if you don't know where that knowledge comes from, and feel a deep desire to offer a helping hand. Please don't feel foolish or think that you are being a "goody-goody".

Just act upon your compassion, act upon your desire to be kind, or selfless, or more aware in general, because that reflex and that knowledge is simply you reconnecting to your original self before life conditioned you.

This last day here in my peaceful abode is really for me, and while I am tempted to keep writing, I feel that for now I really did get something from being alone out here. I am aware that these words might be greeted with cynicism or judgment, but they are

funded by a deep desire to at least open a debate that addresses the sudden changes we all live with in our lives; for generations where interaction has always been a part of who we are, the loss of it is heartbreaking.

I don't think I am alone when I say I miss a lot of things: things like politeness, civility, chivalry, and genuine social graces that we, as the last generations who remember, feel it is our responsibility to preserve.

How that is achieved is not for me to say. What I do know is that if any of us disregard our strength and overlook a bully picking on a man, woman, boy or girl, we are abandoning our social obligation to be compassionate and supportive to each other.

Seeking guidance through ego is like using a GPS system without a satellite, you're going to get lost.

In a small village of one hundred people I am sure there would be no tolerance with regard to selfish non-inclusive behaviour because there would be an understanding that the support of each other is not only in the best interest of the village, but also in the best interest of each and every member of that community.

I had a thought, maybe more of a question, while being here this calm morning on the last day of my peaceful retreat. My question is this: *have you ever imagined or dreamed of a different kind of society - a society where we are kinder, more loving and supportive of each other, regardless of social or financial standing, someone's religion, colour, or sexual preference?*

If you have, I pose the following question: *can you walk and talk like a member of that society, even if that means being misunderstood and questioned as to what your motive might be?*

It might even hurt at times, being regarded with suspicion simply for trying to be more communicative or friendly, but ask yourself this: if you are not one of the contributors for change through action - an action of gratitude, love, peace, and inclusion - then what are you contributing to?

Before I leave the desert and bring this piece of writing to an end, I want to say thank you for allowing me to share my thoughts.

Do know I am aware we all see things differently, and I understand none of these words might impact you in a positive way, but please remember they are written with a desire to encourage, albeit to a small degree, and offer some food for thought

Defining faith
creates war,
yet a silent faith
creates peace.

that might evoke in one's heart an act of kindness which may just be the deciding difference whether someone gives up or not.

These words are written to encourage the pursuit of knowledge that will help all of us, young or old. There is only a motive of good and a desire to say that I myself have been in those dark places, alone, feeling lost without guidance, and I have needed so very much to feel less alone or less misunderstood.

I may not know you personally, but because I care about you and whatever suffering you may have gone through, or may even be experiencing right now, I wish to say... YOU ARE NOT ALONE. There are millions of us, and we can collectively make a difference, even if it means being different for a minute, finding courage to transcend the noise and the seeking of validation.

I meet so many people who simply don't have the energy and time after a long week at work, or weeks of stress over bills and worries, to try and change the world, but a simple commitment to kindness and interactiveness is a great start; it will set into motion a ripple that will eventually become a tsunami of change: change for the better, towards a more conscious world.

Let us consider how love and kindness feels to give or receive, and let us ask ourselves this: when did it become something we don't have time for, and how long do we all feel we can live without it as we go about our daily grind?

Apathy is becoming a norm, let's
make a commitment to kindness,
it can change the world

Nothing will change all by itself; it needs us to do that. Sure, we have all read books that encourage this idea, but without at least an occasional effort from all of us, how can we expect change?

Life is brief and eventually we will all leave this Earth; that is something that is absolute.

But between our first inhale and our last exhale, try to remember this:

"It is a blessing to be a blessing"

With love.

Special thanks to

Lazy Sky Retreat

Lightning Source UK Ltd.
Milton Keynes UK
UKHW02n1356280218
318561UK00003BB/24/P

9 781910 705988